Pieces of a Reverie

Rié Max Dolden

BookLeaf Publishing

India | USA | UK

Presentation by *BookLeaf Publishing*

Web: www.bookleafpub.com

E-mail: info@bookleafpub.com

ISBN: 9789358318111

First edition 2023

ACKNOWLEDGEMENT

I am eternally grateful and give a wholehearted thanks to my family who have consistently provided a safety blanket of patience, understanding and reassurance as I went through this journey.
I am truly blessed.

PREFACE

I wanted to mark an important milestone birthday in the most profound way, so I entered Bookleaf's Publishing Competition. I'd been lost in my thoughts leading up to my birthday, a moment of reflection and thought it would be a great time to put those thoughts into pieces of prose.

I'm a constant daydreamer, I don't believe you have to be asleep to dream, being wide awake provides a wide range of possibilities and this collection of poems conveys the emotion, the sight of nature and all that it is to be human.

Cloud

When worries etch your face
The wrinkles are here to stay
Don't look away
Allow your face to be kissed by the sun
And the clouds, a cushion for your cheeks
When a love of daydreaming is spun from
looking at the clouds
Know that an appreciation grows
And the secret lies in every cloud
For there's a silver lining in everything

You

You who came into my life
With such ease and clarity
Shook my world full force
You took me out of my dark depths
Where I thought I'd stay
But you were the blessing
That I prayed
You whom I love with all my heart
You whom I'll never part
You.

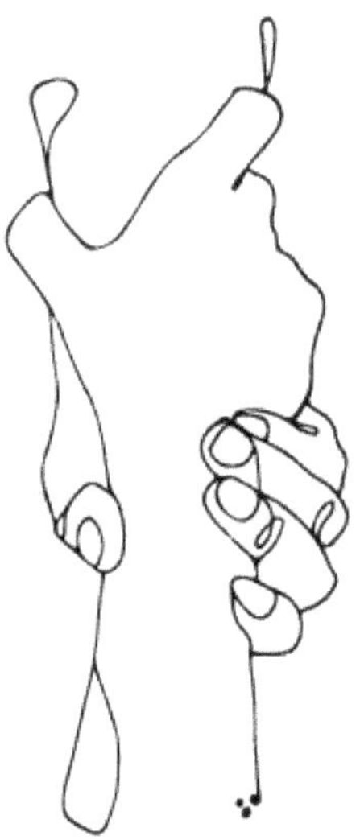

Bus Shelter

Underneath the bus shelter
Rain follows like a Helter-skelter
Down it goes, a wayward journey
As the cycle goes round and round
The rain falls, staccato overhead
I shiver with cold
As damp seeps through to my bones
People clamber together
With warmth on their mind
As rain continues to fall like luminous confetti
Does it dawn on me
The wait will be a while
Underneath this bus shelter

Blur

The days all blur into one when my thoughts of
you submerge
I'm drowning in your waters and holding out for
your hand
Yet, you're nowhere in sight
Leaving me to gasp for breath as I sink below
the surface
I miss you, I miss you so much
But there's nothing left of us
Just memories of a time we spent together

And as the water seeps into my lungs
I don't fight it
I let it fill me to capacity

I'd rather drown in self pity, then live with
knowing
You no longer love me

The darkness of the water engulfs me
The depth of my sadness is grave
I should have been more vocal
But it's too late, too late for trying and expecting
for miracles

Lay You To Rest

The grass grew
Since the last time I was here
The blazing sun turned it to straw, I almost
passed you by
If it weren't for the gifts that have been
weathered by rain
But remain untouched
On your gravestone
Your smile when you saw me for what I was
Is a memory that breaks me
But a memory that drives my sanity
When days get tough.

Where are you now?
In the clouds watching over me, telling me to get
over it
I'm consumed by you day and night

And all I want is to feel your light
To once again feel like my life isn't falling apart
But i know, I have to lay you to rest
Lay you to rest

I Will

Take my hand
Hold on to it tight
I will make the shadows disappear
And surround you with sunlight
I will stay by your side
When Life brings you down
When you feel like it's not worth living
I will make it right
I will cast away your demons
With strong words of love and nurture
I will take it upon myself
To show you that's the will of being
Friends who stick together
And never falter

Align

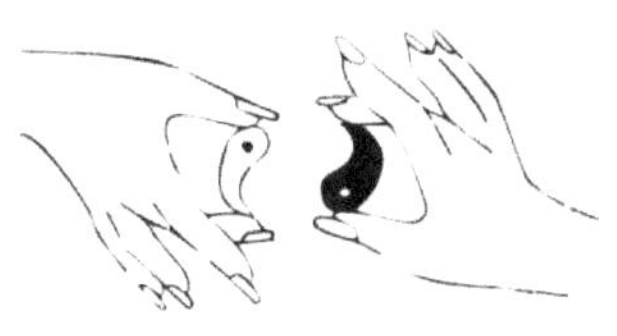

They say, when you feel lost
Look to the stars
As they pave a way
To map out your destiny
The stars, they glisten and glimmer
And most importantly
Listen
To your dreams, your insecurities
Your inner most feelings, you dare not whisper
Out loud for another to hear
When your darkest days feel
The Loneliest
Please know, you're never alone
Not really
Not ever

This Side of Heaven

I touch the mirror to check you can see me
That you're on the other side
Tracing my fingers with yours
I look at my reflection staring back at me
But I'm looking outwards
Hoping you still see me
On this side of Heaven

The Beach

We both stand with our feet in the sand
The feel of the moist sand grains filter through
Exfoliating my feet making them brand new
Around us the heat is all encompassing
As it stifles me with it's humidity
We stroll to the water as the waves crash to
shore
And the intensity of the ocean is what my mind
Adores
A fresh perspective and a chance at something
new
Is all that's needed to ward off the blues

The Scenery

The Church where my parents were married
Stood on the hill of a backdrop of green valleys
Where the sunshine filtered through the clouds
Looked like a picture of the heavens
A picture perfect moment
Idyllic in nature and heartfelt emotions
Love like this lasted forever
So they say, as two people come together
On a day in November

Joke

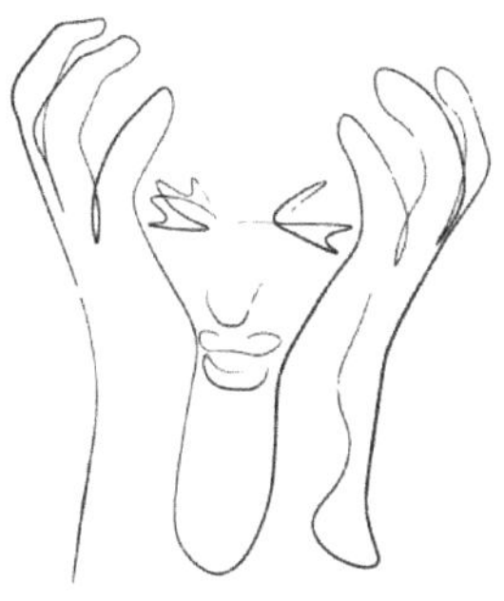

The joke was on me
It started out so beautifully
In a way where a random conversation
Blossomed unexpectedly
And time collided and blurred into one
I looked forward to early mornings
Just to hear how your evenings were going
And time stood still
The acknowledgement that I was a mere pawn
In this game, where my heart is now torn
I believe it now to be a life of lies
Where I was the only one who thought
We would stand the test of time
But the jokes on me
The jokes on me

Piano

And as I sit in front of the keyboard
My life has played out amongst the keys
I wonder how it all came to be
The melodies that were in my head
Were the hardships I battled through
Now they are stories made of music
From rhythm and blues
And as I sit in front of the keyboard
The rush of emotions are on the forefront
Of these keys, the keys that have shaped
The melodies about me.

Rise

I will no longer grieve
I will no longer wallow in self pity nor regret
I will no longer look at old photos
And swear again
I refuse to feel bad for my reactions
I refuse to back down from situations
I refuse to follow society's norms
And I will rise, rise above it all
Break free and be the best version you'll ever see
Of Me.

A Dream

You came to life from desperate dreams
Dreams that were spun from loneliness
A reverie that had manifested from nightmares
All my aches and heartbreak
They disappeared for a while
I lived in fantasy of being loved wholeheartedly
Where I felt protected
And shielded from reality
I clung to you, like a life raft
In hopes we'd float into the sunset
Like all fantasies and happy endings
You were mine for some time

Tears

Tears flow down sad faces
Pooling at the feet
Building up to a river towards the sea
No one says sadness is measured
Like happiness is sunshine
Just salty tears and a puffy face

Confidence

Confidence is not something that is brought
And paid for by a credit card
Even though the expectation is if you buy into a
lifestyle
You're rolling in an ego
Manufactured by commodities
That are screaming for your attention
All of life is a mere reflection
On what is deemed greedy
Confidence

Glow

Let the air settle
As the sun breaks through the clouds
Illuminating the cornflower blue skies with
blush pinks, mellow yellows and zesty oranges
Allow the scene to radiate through the air beams
An ever glow to herald the start of a new day
A new day of opportunity
To bask in the simplicity of nature's free luxuries

Abundance

Give me the world
I want nothing less
If I strive for the Earth
I might as well take all The Planets
In this Universe
And as infinity knows no bounds
Count the stars with me
As we hold hands
As we travel through the lifespan
Of this galaxy.
You are the abundance that thrives within me

Thirst

Leave me wanting
Don't skip on anything
I want you to take it slow
Open your senses
And feel intoxicated
This is what thirst feels like
You take a sip, drip
You'd want to take it all in
Baby, I'll make you want me
Until you'll be basking in Forever and ever

Mine

You are mine
As I am yours
As the Noctilucent Clouds
Pass through the night
Everything is where it should be
Given day or night
My love is painted in nature
As I write

A Gentle Reminder

A feather left behind
From an angel left in sight
A gentle reminder
You are never alone
Even at times, it feels so

A floral fragrance
Clings to the air
A gentle reminder
A family member was there

A cool breeze, a dip in temperature
My skin reacts
A gentle reminder
A love pact to never surrender

9 789358 318111